Yuc

Disgusting Things That Are Surprisingly Useful

T0337327

Contents

Written by Mio Debnam

Collins

Yuck – germs!

Chances are, you've washed your hands recently. Scientists tell us that washing hands with soap and water stops nasty germs from entering our bodies and making us sick. But ... what exactly are "germs"?

Germs are simple **organisms** – or living things. They are so small that they cannot be seen with our eyes alone. There are several different groups of germs. Two groups are bacteria and moulds. Some types of bacteria and mould can make us sick, but others are really important for our health.

Most bacteria are harmless to humans, which is lucky, as they are so common that if you had super-powerful eyes and X-ray vision, you'd see them everywhere – including on and inside our bodies!

3

Bad bacteria

Have you ever fallen over and cut yourself? Normally, if you clean the wound, it heals by itself.

Sometimes, however, the wound becomes swollen, red and full of yellow pus – that's the white blood cells in your body fighting the bad bacteria.

Your body is really good at fighting germs, but on rare occasions, you may need help to make sure the bacteria doesn't make you ill.

If that happens, a doctor will give you medicine called an antibiotic to fight the **infection**, kill the bacteria and make you well again.

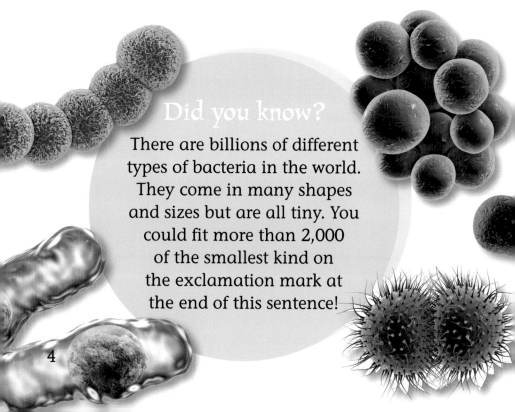

Did you know?

There are billions of different types of bacteria in the world. They come in many shapes and sizes but are all tiny. You could fit more than 2,000 of the smallest kind on the exclamation mark at the end of this sentence!

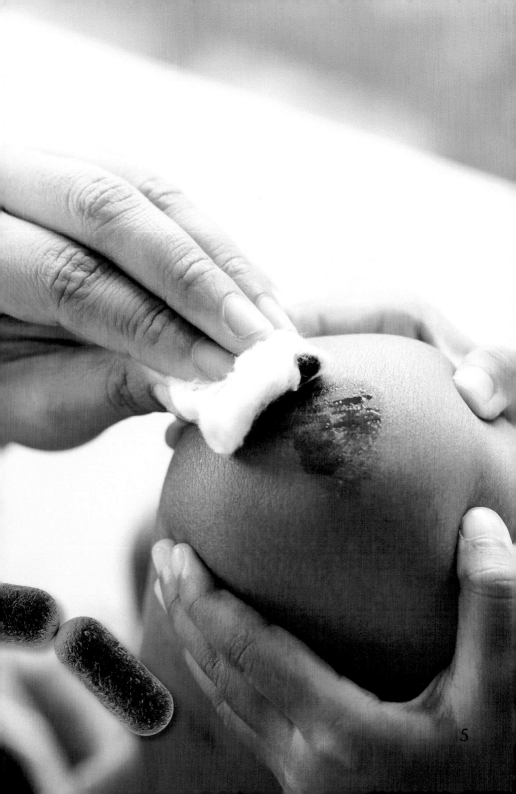

Good bacteria in the body

A human adult has about 250 grams of good bacteria living in their **guts**!

We need gut bacteria because, without it, we wouldn't be able to **digest** our food.

Good bacteria live in many parts of our body. They stop bad bacteria from growing, so they protect us. They also help to make our **immune system** stronger, so we can stay healthy.

Did you know?

250 grams of bacteria is the same weight as three lemons.

6

good versus bad bacteria

stomach

guts

Good bacteria at work

... in food production

Without good bacteria, we wouldn't be able to make certain foods, such as yoghurt, cheese, soy sauce, pickles, vinegar, and many other tasty things.

... in the garden

Different good bacteria help break down things like fallen leaves in the forest, and your kitchen scraps in compost heaps. They turn these waste products into new soil, full of the **nutrients** plants need to grow.

... in sewage plants

Good bacteria are also used to treat the human waste and water that we flush down toilets and drains. The bacteria added to the dirty water tanks in **sewage plants** help to make clean water. This can then be released into the ocean or into rivers.

Bad mould

Have you ever seen fruit or bread covered in blue, green, red or white fuzz?

Or perhaps you've seen black or green powder growing on walls, on books, or on furniture?

Both the powder and the fuzz are different types of mould.

People dislike mould because some types can make you ill. If you spend time in a room where mould is growing, you may breathe it in. If you do, you may get headaches, a cough, sore eyes, or a rash.

Eating mouldy food can give you a stomachache.

11

Bad versus good mould

Generally, if you see mould on your food you shouldn't eat it, but some cheeses depend on special types of mould to give them the flavour and smell they're famous for.

Next time you're food shopping, look for soft cheese covered in a white, almost fluffy coat, such as goat's cheese or Brie.

Brie

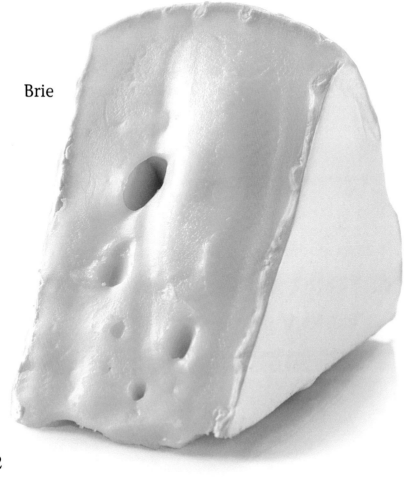

Next look for a "blue cheese", such as Stilton.
It's called "blue cheese" because there are blue lines
running through the cheese.

Both the white coat covering Brie, and the blue lines
in Stilton are moulds growing on or in the cheese!
These moulds are different from the mould that causes
food to spoil, and are safe to eat.

Stilton

Lifesaving mould

One hundred years ago, if you became unwell because of bad bacteria, there weren't any good medicines to help you get well. Many people died when they got a bacterial infection.

Then, in 1928, doctor and scientist, Alexander Fleming made an amazing discovery.

Did you know?

If your doctor has ever given you medicine for a bad sore throat or an earache, then you've probably had an antibiotic!

Alexander Fleming in his lab

Fleming noticed that when a certain type of mould happened to land on the bacteria he was studying, the bacteria died. Scientists studied the mould to see how it was killing the bacteria, and this led to them developing a new kind of medicine – called antibiotics.

The first antibiotic, which Fleming had helped to discover, is called penicillin. Since then, many other antibiotics have been developed, and countless lives have been saved!

Most adults would tell you that insects such as mosquitoes and termites are annoying and sometimes dangerous and destructive …
and creepy-crawlies like locusts, mealworms and beetles are often greeted with disgust!

But if you look a bit closer, you'll discover that insects are interesting and sometimes useful!

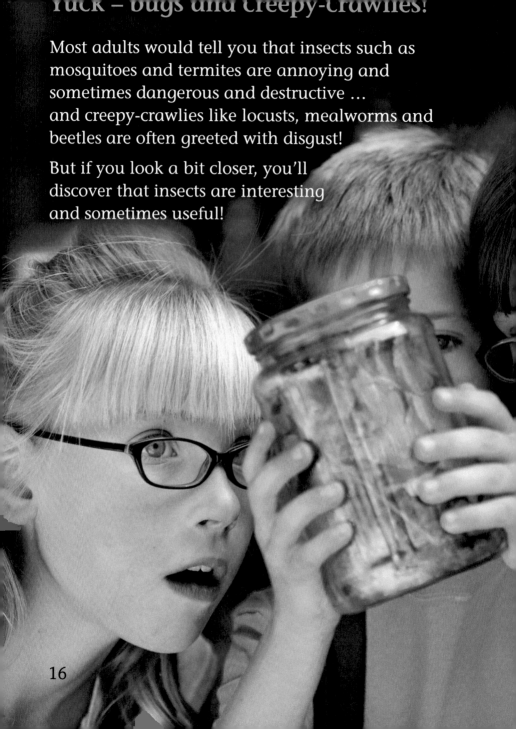

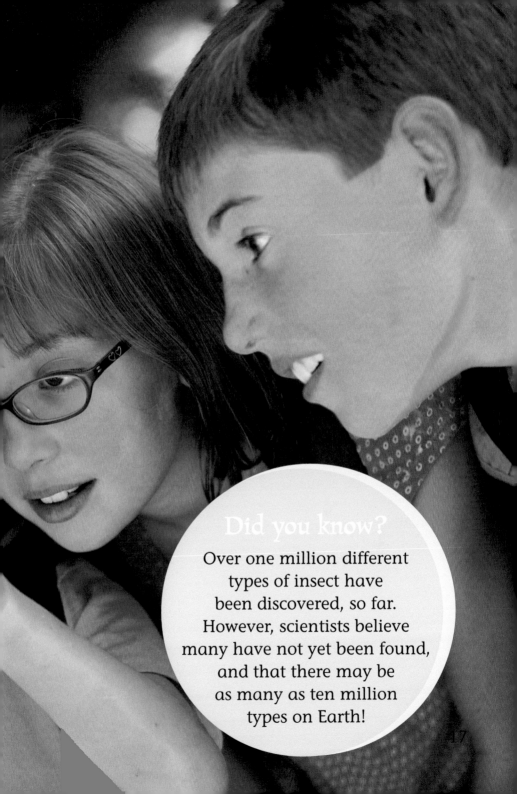

Did you know?

Over one million different
types of insect have
been discovered, so far.
However, scientists believe
many have not yet been found,
and that there may be
as many as ten million
types on Earth!

17

Mosquitoes

These bloodsucking insects are unpopular worldwide. Mosquito bites are often really itchy! Also, some mosquitoes can carry and pass on diseases when they bite.

Many people spray pesticide – a liquid that is poisonous to mosquitoes – in gardens and grassy areas where mosquitoes rest, to kill them. However, pesticides also kill helpful and harmless insects such as bees, ladybirds and butterflies.

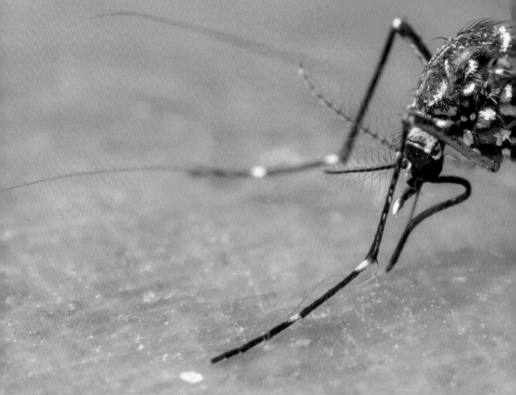

Bee-friendly ways to not get bitten

Mosquitoes lay eggs in water, so change
the water in birdbaths and pet water bowls
every day so the eggs won't have a chance to
hatch. To prevent being bitten, use a natural
repellent spray containing citronella, wear long
sleeves and trousers or use a mosquito net.

Did you know that a male mosquito never bites? Both the male and female mosquito can live on nectar and water alone. However, a female mosquito needs to feed on blood when she's about to lay eggs as she needs the nutrients in blood to make the eggs.

adult mosquito drinking nectar from a flower

Mosquitoes are annoying and can be dangerous to humans, but they're important for the creatures that eat them! Mosquito babies (called larvae) live in water and are food for fish. Adult mosquitoes are food for all sorts of birds, bats and spiders.

In addition, like bees, mosquitoes help to **pollinate** many plants, when they visit flowers to eat nectar.

mosquito larvae in water

Termites

Termites are small, ant-like insects that live in large groups called colonies. They can be very destructive, making holes in wooden things, such as houses and furniture.

However, many types – or **species** – of termite are amazing builders, and farmers!

Some termite species build a huge clay mound over their underground home. Larger mounds can be nine metres high – that's the height of three elephants on top of each other!

Termites need to keep their homes cool and moist, or the mushrooms they farm for food won't grow.

They build special tunnels in the mound, so air from outside will be pulled in and flow past some mud, which cools it. This fresh, cooled air pushes out the stale hot air and keeps the inside of the mound cool.

a large termite mound

In Zimbabwe, Africa, where it's hot by day, but cooler at night, one of the largest buildings in the country has been built using termite design ideas!

Most modern buildings have big windows and smooth, flat walls, but the Eastgate Centre doesn't!

Like termite mounds, the walls are "bumpy" and very thick. They soak up the heat during the day, stopping the inside of the building from getting too hot. At night, the spiky design helps the walls to quickly get rid of all the stored heat.

The Eastgate Centre also uses termite "natural air-conditioning" ideas, to pull in fresh, cool air and get rid of hot air.

This allows the people inside to stay cool during the day and warm at night, and saves lots of electricity and money!

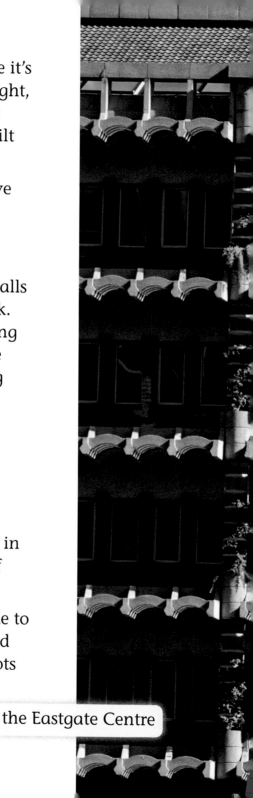

the Eastgate Centre

Insects eating our food

Many insects eat **crops** both when they're growing and after harvest, when they're stored.

One common pest is the locust – a type of grasshopper that gathers in big groups called swarms. A swarm can cover an area larger than London, UK, and contains billions of locusts.

a locust swarm

locust

Swarms can quickly travel large distances, eating all the crops, wild plants and grass in their path, causing the animals and humans who depend on those plants, to starve.

Other insects, like the mealworm beetle and its young, attack crops after they've been harvested. They often live in and eat grains, such as wheat and oats, stored on farms, and occasionally they can be found in dried food in people's homes, too.

mealworms

Insects as our food

Humans have eaten insects for hundreds of years – because some people find them tasty and good for you.

You might think that's yucky, but insects are close relatives of shrimps, prawns and lobsters – which many people love to eat.

It takes less land, less water and less electricity to raise enough insects (such as locusts or mealworms) for us to eat, than it does to raise an animal (such as a cow) for its meat, so it's better for our planet too.

Insects can be eaten whole or ground up into flour. In Asia, cooked insects are popular snacks in food markets, and in Europe, food made from insects can be found in supermarkets – such as insect biscuits and burgers!

Would you eat an insect burger?

Yuck – human waste!

When you use the toilet, you flush and forget it.

Good riddance – human waste, both liquid and solid, smells bad and is full of things your body wants to get rid of. It can carry disease-causing germs, too.

The water and waste you flush down the toilet, together with the water that goes down the drain when you have a bath or a shower, is called "raw sewage".

Raw sewage has to be treated and cleaned so it doesn't pollute the environment. It's filtered to separate the solids from the liquid. The liquid is treated until it is clean. Then it is released into a river or the sea. But, what about the solid waste?

Surprisingly, people have found many interesting uses for it!

Solid bodily waste as plant food

Plants need food (nutrients) to grow – which they get from the soil. Farmers regularly add **fertiliser** to soil to feed their crops.

In the past, solid waste from humans, birds, bats and farm animals was added directly to the soil as fertiliser. However, fresh waste is smelly, contains germs, and eating vegetables and fruit that still have traces of waste on them can make you sick. So these days, using fresh bodily waste is not common. Instead, it's treated to get rid of the smell and make it safe to use.

Did you know?

Solid waste (dung) from farm animals, when used as fertiliser, is called manure.

Solid waste from bats and birds, used as fertiliser, is called guano.

Solid waste from humans, used as fertiliser, is called night soil.

Solid bodily waste as fuel

In the past, dried solid waste from cows, goats and horses was burnt to heat homes, and to cook with. This still happens in some places, but burning waste is smelly and smoky.

These days, farm animal waste can be turned into biogas, which is a fuel. The waste is mixed with good bacteria in large covered tanks. The bacteria breaks down the waste to release the gas.

In Kenya, Africa, many trees are cut down to make charcoal to cook with. A company there has invented a way to use human waste as fuel. They heat treat it and mix it with other things, such as sawdust, to turn it into dry lumps, which look like BBQ briquettes! These "waste briquettes" don't smell, are germ-free, and burn well. Using them means fewer trees have to be cut down, which is good for the environment.

drying cow dung for fuel

35

Building with solid human waste

Every year, mountains of solid human waste are collected at sewage plants. This human waste is often burnt and the ash is buried in rubbish landfills.

Inventors worldwide have been trying to find a use for the ash, as landfills are getting full.

Several groups have found that when the ash is mixed with other materials, such as sand, clay or concrete, strong bricks can be made.

Bricks using human waste are being made in several countries. In the UK the solid waste of four million people is collected at the Beckton sewage plant. This is recycled to make two million strong, clean bricks a year – enough bricks to build thousands of houses and apartments.

Clay bricks like this may become less common in the future, if bio-bricks made from waste become more popular!

Civet coffee

One of the rarest, most expensive types of coffee bean is found in the solid bodily waste of the Asian palm civet cat!

civet cat with coffee cherries

Coffee is made from the roasted seeds, or "coffee beans", of a fruit called the coffee cherry. Civet cats eat the fruit, but the seeds aren't digested, and come out whole in the animals' waste.

Did you know?

In the past, farmers hunted in the forest for the solid bodily waste of wild civet cats. These days, coffee farmers catch and place civet cats in cages to make collecting their waste easier.

People pick up the waste, wash it off the coffee beans, roast the beans, and then use them to make "kopi luwak", which many coffee fans say tastes better than normal coffee.

roasted beans

cleaned beans

civet cat poo containing coffee beans

39

Drinking liquid human waste!

Have you ever wondered where astronauts get their food and water from?

Space missions often last a few months. Everything astronauts need, including food and water, has to be carried to Space from Earth.

But ... because water weighs a lot, they can't carry enough to last the whole trip, so it has to be recycled from their sweat and liquid waste!

The International Space Station (ISS) has a system which gathers sweat, the liquid waste from the toilet, and any other waste water, and turns it, again and again, into pure water which can be used for drinking or for cleaning!

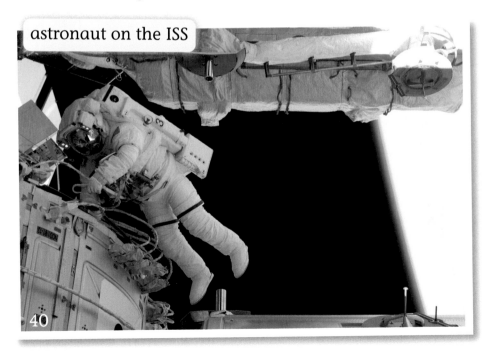

astronaut on the ISS

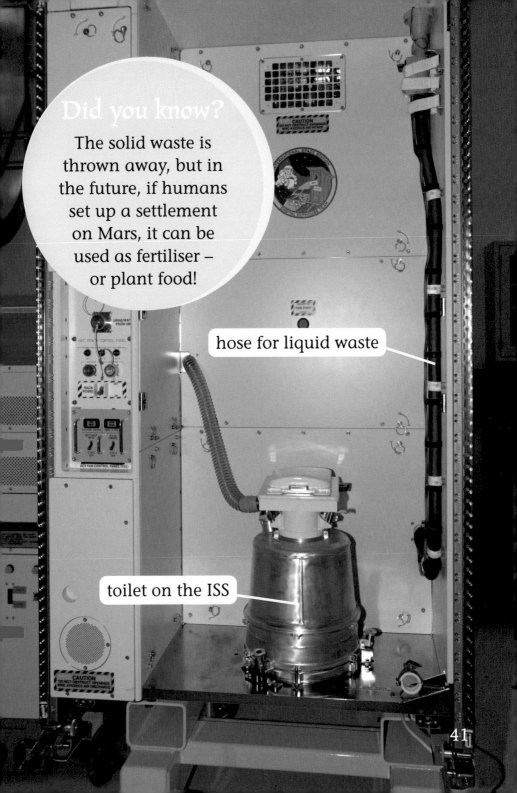

Did you know?

The solid waste is thrown away, but in the future, if humans set up a settlement on Mars, it can be used as fertiliser – or plant food!

hose for liquid waste

toilet on the ISS

Disease detectives

In 2019, a germ that causes a disease called COVID-19 started spreading. Millions of people became **infected** with, or caught, it.

Some infected people became very sick, while others felt completely fine but were "hidden carriers". You could easily catch COVID-19 by being close to someone infected, whether they felt sick or not.

It became important to find out where the infected people were, and how fast COVID-19 was spreading, so that governments knew when lockdowns and extra testing were necessary.

Luckily, the human waste of all infected people, even hidden carriers, contain the germ. So scientists tested the raw sewage in many different areas, to find the places where large numbers of people were infected. By doing this, they were able to help control the spread of COVID-19!

testing sewage water

43

Glossary

crops plants farmed by people, such as vegetables and grains

digest when our bodies break down food, to give us energy and nutrients we need to live

fertiliser soil food for plants

guts our stomachs and intestines – where food is digested

immune system part of our body that fights germs and keeps us healthy

infection/infected when a germ enters your body and makes you unwell

nutrients things in food that help your body work well and give you energy

organisms every living thing from bacteria, to plants, to birds, to humans

pollinate spread pollen from flower to flower, so that plants can produce fruit

sewage plants places that collect and treat dirty water from toilets and drains

species a group of very similar organisms, which are different from other groups: for example, tigers are one species, lions are another, though they're both big cats

Index

Good vs bad

Bacteria

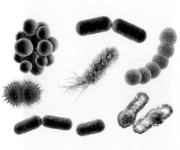

Mould

Mosquitoes

Why is it bad?

Disease-causing bacteria makes you ill.

Some moulds can make you ill.

itchy bites, can pass disease

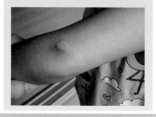

Why is it good?

helps us digest food and fight bad bacteria,
used to make some foods, for example, yoghurt, breaks down waste products

needed to make some cheese, needed to make antibiotics

food for other creatures, pollinates flowers

Termites	Locusts and mealworms	Human waste

destroy wooden things	eat our crops	is smelly, contains germs

using termite design ideas in buildings saves electricity	good source of food for humans, eating insects is good for the environment	useful as: fertiliser, fuel, bricks, makes special coffee! liquid waste recycled to clean water, useful to detect disease

Ideas for reading

Written by Christine Whitney
Primary Literacy Consultant

Reading objectives:
- be introduced to non-fiction books that are structured in different ways
- listen to, discuss and express views about non-fiction
- retrieve and record information from non-fiction
- discuss and clarify the meanings of words

Spoken language objectives:
- participate in discussion
- speculate, hypothesise, imagine and explore ideas through talk
- ask relevant questions

Curriculum links: Science: The importance for humans of hygiene; Writing: Write for different purposes

Word count: 2936

Interest words: bacteria, infection, mould, nutrients, sewage, human waste, fertiliser

Resources: Paper and pencils, assorted building blocks

Build a context for reading

- Before children see the book, ask them what they understand by the word *Yuck!* When is it used and why?
- Ask children to look at the front cover of the book and to make predictions regarding the content. Ask for a volunteer to explain the meaning of *Disgusting Things That Are Surprisingly Useful.*
- Now turn to the back cover and read the blurb. Ask children to discuss what they think they will find on the contents page.
- Introduce the words *sewage* and *human waste* to the group. You may wish to have a short discussion with the group about the latter phrase. Ensure children understand that it does not simply refer to rubbish that goes in the bin.

Understand and apply reading strategies

- Turn to the contents page and ask children to find three different sections in the book. The first section is called *Yuck – germs!* What are the other two sections called?